KU-484-478

The Sayings of the
BUDDHA

Reflections for every day

ARCTURUS

ARCTURUS

This edition published in 2018 by Arcturus Publishing Limited
26/27 Bickels Yard, 151–153 Bermondsey Street,
London SE1 3HA

Copyright © Arcturus Holdings Limited

All rights reserved. No part of this publication may be reproduced,
stored in a retrieval system, or transmitted, in any form or by any means,
electronic, mechanical, photocopying, recording or otherwise, without
prior written permission in accordance with the provisions of the
Copyright Act 1956 (as amended). Any person or persons who do any
unauthorised act in relation to this publication may be liable to criminal
prosecution and civil claims for damages.

ISBN: 978-1-78950-096-7
AD006959UK

Printed in China

CONTENTS

Introduction 4

Life of the Buddha......................6

His Teaching 14

The Sayings..................................24

Introduction

Buddhism is considered to be one of the most important world faiths and it certainly has its influence on the spiritual life of the planet. It is estimated that half the countries of the world have been directly influenced by Buddhist thinking. How many practising Buddhists actually exist on the face of the globe is hard to estimate, but what is evident is that the power of Buddhism to capture the imagination of the human mind is as strong today as it was when the Buddha gave his doctrine of 'The Middle Way' to a gathering of five men who had been his original followers in the Deer Park in Saranath in about 450 BC.

This was a teaching that he himself thought long and hard about before delivering because he thought it so subtle and demanding that few would be able to follow, and yet, here in a time in which materialism is said to govern our thinking, the power of this man's spiritual realization still has a profound influence, and a growing one, particularly as far as the West is concerned. This says a lot about what this one man discovered in deep meditation. It also says a lot about us as human beings. Are his words of such forceful influence because they speak directly to something which all of us hold within us and in our more penetrating moments dimly realize?

An answer to this question can only be discovered if we devote time to a consideration of what he realized in his own life and sought to express in the years he spent teaching.

This book contains a range of aphorisms which express in different ways the core doctrines of Buddhism. They are derived mainly from the Pali Canon, written in the first century BC. This is a collection of manuscripts which recorded in writing the words of the Buddha that had previously been passed on orally. Also contained in the book are extracts of other works which hold a central position in the vast outpouring of the human spirit which constitutes Buddhist literature.

Life of the Buddha

So what do we know about this man called the 'Buddha'? The first thing we have to realize is that this is not so much a name as an indication of his state of being. The Buddha is a title given to somebody of the highest spiritual understanding. It means 'One Who is Awake'. He is awake not in the way that we normally understand being awake. We are awake only to a dream of life within which we seek to create an identity. What this man was awake to was spiritual reality, things as they are in truth.

His name was Siddhartha Gautama. He was born in 487 BC in Lumbini, a state that spanned the border of modern-day Nepal and Northern India. He was born into the Kshatriya, the warrior caste, part of a ruling family. His father was determined to provide for his son: legend has it that Siddhartha was raised in a palace surrounded by high walls to prevent him from witnessing the suffering that is part of human experience.

His mother had a dream on conception that a white baby elephant entered her side. From this the seers predicted that Siddhartha would one day be either a great political or religious leader. We can only speculate as to whether or not his father was trying to shield him from the pain and suffering that can easily be central to the human lot. This seems likely, especially given that Siddhartha's own mother died when he was only seven days old. Another possibility is that in the light of the seers' prediction his father was concerned that one day Siddhartha would give up his privileged life and seek spiritual enlightenment as a way of transcending the sorrows of this world. Whatever the reason for his action, at the age of 29 Siddhartha slipped away in the night to become a wandering monk.

Before this Siddhartha had been raised with all the advantages his status in society was able to provide. At the age of 16 he was married to the beautiful Yahodra who bore him a son, Rahula. Despite the luxury of his life, this intelligent and sensitive man felt a lack; there was a spiritual understanding that wasn't available to him.

Later legend states that all of this came to a climax with four journeys he took out of the palace. On the first one of these, his father, determined to protect his son, arranged for the streets to be filled with happy and healthy people. He had all the old and infirm removed from view, but as chance would have it one remained undetected. When Siddhartha saw this, he commanded his charioteer to return to the palace in order to reflect upon what it meant to grow old. In his second journey he encountered a sick man and on the third a funeral procession. All this inevitably led him to ponder upon the transient nature of human existence, which no amount of privilege could protect him from. On his fourth journey he spoke to a holy man, a conversation which sowed in him the belief that it was possible to find a spiritual solution to what today we call existential misery.

Whether this legend is true or not, what is evident is that what he was facing in his life were the questions which we have all considered in some way. How do we find fulfilment in life? How do we overcome the pain that can so easily be our lot? What is the meaning of human existence and how might we discover the Truth? For Siddhartha, these questions were so pressing that he stole away in the middle of the night, left his family, his wife and child and renounced the world.

Wandering monks who had turned their back on worldly life were a familiar part of Indian life, as they are to this very day, in a land where schools of philosophy and gurus of various kinds abound. Siddhartha's first teacher, Ajara Kalama, taught him meditational techniques which encouraged ever deeper insight. His nature was such that he quickly mastered the techniques and achieved what was known as 'the sphere of nothingness'. Although such techniques granted more than a touch of bliss, the pain and suffering he encountered in the world as we know it remained regardless of the ease of mind discovered during meditation.

Siddhartha went on to study under Uddaka Ramaputta, who taught him techniques which allowed him to enter ever finer states, including the one described as 'the sphere of neither perception nor non-perception'. He recognized the validity of these states, but he also realized, sublime as they were, they were not what he was seeking.

After this he turned to austerity as a means of discovering that which he sought. He first developed breath control techniques which were based on reducing the intake of air, so much so that in practising these techniques it became possible to hardly breathe at all.

He then began reducing his intake of food. He carried this through until he was existing on one spoon of bean soup a day. For six years he practised these austerities, determined that through them he would achieve the enlightenment which he was seeking. What he discovered instead was that a life of extreme asceticism not only took its inevitable toll on his body but gave him nothing of what he was questing after. He came to the conclusion that rather than pursuing these extreme attempts to achieve realization, the only solution was to adopt what he came to describe as the 'Middle Way', neither over- indulgence nor self-mortification.

When he had come to this conclusion the small band of followers who had attached themselves to him over the years felt that he had turned his back on the path upon which they were depending upon him to lead them, and deserted him.

He was left to himself with no one to support him, his family gone, his followers gone, his reputation as man of insight and understanding ruined. Entirely alone, he was determined on one thing, the goal that he had always set himself: to cut through the maya, the veil of ignorance, and discover life's central reality, the source of true understanding.

It was at this point that a childhood memory came to mind. It was of his father ploughing whilst Siddhartha sat in the shade of a rose-apple tree. The steady measure of the ox-team, the play of sunlight and shade had allowed him so easily to slip below the surface of life and discover, unlooked for, what he now so desperately sought. Was 'Enlightenment' easy, so natural to man that it was child's play? Was he in all his desperate determination missing out on what was immediately to hand?

As this thought arose, he made up his mind that regardless of what was granted him, he would not take another step in this life until he found what he sought. He sat beneath a large, spreading tree and entered into meditation. In the course of one night he achieved the goal he had set himself, spiritual awakening. Having overcome the force of worldly temptation, he, through contemplation, obtained knowledge of the continual cycle of lives, not only those that he had encountered personally but also the lives of all as they rose and fell. He saw how people forged their own lives, of how they were subject to their own actions. He saw the direct link between craving and suffering. He saw his own identity dissolve into the totality of being, the source of true understanding. In the final watch of the night he attained full enlightenment. It was at this point that Siddhartha Gautama became the Buddha. He awoke from the dream of life and became enlightened.

For seven weeks he remained, reflecting on what had been revealed to him, wondering if there was any possibility that the insight he had been granted could ever be communicated. His first thought was that he should remain in seclusion, but the compassion for which the Buddha became renowned dictated that he should return to the world, to teach and devote the rest of his life to 'Turning the Wheel of the Law'. He walked the hundred miles to Saranath, seeking the five men who had deserted him. If they could be made to understand, there was the chance that others might be made to understand as well. He found them in the Deer Park in Saranath.

When they saw him their first response was to reject him. They were determined on a path of extreme asceticism, and they saw only what they considered to be his weakness. Even so there was something about this man that was undeniably powerful, and despite themselves they entered into a debate. Slowly they began to understand. They began to see what he had seen. Over days, not only by the power of his teaching, but also by the power of his presence, one by one, he led them to a state of Enlightenment.

From this he knew that others could also be led to understanding, and having made a spiritual journey he commenced a physical one, a journey which would last for forty-five years, during which time he wandered from place to place teaching, his brotherhood, or sangha, growing and growing, with more and more men and women coming to achieve what he had achieved. Buddhism speaks of what can be understood and known when there is a determination to go beyond the world as it is usually experienced, when there is a determination to arise out of the sleep of life and achieve what the Buddha described as Nirvana.

His Teaching

So what were the truths that the Buddha managed to convince his first five followers of in the Deer Park? At the heart of this discourse were what became known as the Four Noble Truths. These take the form of a formal medical diagnosis as to the mass of ill that is associated with life. As with all medical assessment it consists of diagnosis and treatment. Life is suffering. Suffering is caused by craving. There can be an end to suffering. There is a way that leads to the end of suffering.

The first of these Truths explores how life has about it an essential suffering, not only the obvious suffering caused by disease and death, but also the suffering caused by loss: the loss of one's loved ones, the loss of those things that one holds dear.

It pointed out that even when one is in possession of something there is the fear of loss. We strive and strain to get what we want and then fear to lose. All this involves suffering.

What the Buddha claims is that the five elements that constitute the individual all have inherent within them the element of suffering. The five elements to which he refers are the physical body, sensation and feeling, cognition, individual characteristics and consciousness.

Clearly what is being referred to here are the constituent elements which go to make this so-called individual. To the Buddha all of these are not so much a hierarchy of elements, more a series of dependencies, none of which can stand by itself alone. Every part is reliant on every other part rather than gathered round a personal identity, or soul. There is nothing left to cling to as some kind of separate self. With a conclusion of this kind the individual is forced to give way. It is in fact blown away, and this is the literal meaning of the word nirvana.

The second of the four Noble Truths identifies the source of suffering as craving. The first of these cravings is the strong desire for all that is pleasant in life, the thirst for sensual satisfaction, with the mind constantly fixed on achieving ways of gaining that satisfaction. The second craving is for life itself, the desire to cling on and possess. The third is the opposite, the desire to reject, revile and finally to destroy. This desire can at best take the form of aversion to those things that we find unpleasant, at worst to an entirely destructive attitude to life out of which arises a whole range of criticism, and general negativity. Inevitably there is something that lies at the heart of all this desire and aversion, a forceful sense of self-identification, the ego and all its conflicting demands.

The Third Noble Truth makes it quite clear that there is a cure from this mass of suffering, and that cure is the direct result of the ending of craving by renouncing it, rejecting it, by non-attachment to it. When the bond is broken, freedom arises. This is clearly a path of self-abnegation, and it is the little self, the realm of me and mine, that according to the Buddha's course of treatment needs to be dissolved. This act of dissolution is nirvana. As his was not a philosophy of attainment – in fact the attempt to try and seize something as a personal possession, does nothing, according to the Buddha, but reinforce the separate self – he would not be drawn as to what lay beyond, but the blissful expression on the face of countless images of the meditating Buddha gives an indication of what occurs when the confines of the heart and mind give way.

What are these confines? The Buddha said they were greed, hatred and delusion. When these are dissolved then the truth is revealed, love is revealed and generosity of spirit is revealed. These are not to be sought for and grasped by some imaginary individual. They naturally arise when this little self is laid down.

Within the Fourth Noble Truth is an outline of the treatment prescribed by the Buddha to bring about the end of suffering. This treatment involves the development of the following: Right View, Right Resolve, Right Speech, Right Action, Right Livelihood, Right Effort, Right Mindfulness, Right Meditation. All of this constitutes the Middle Way, the path in life in which the extremes of excessive indulgence and excessive austerity are avoided. This is the path that leads out of delusion towards the truth.

The word 'path' suggests a journey, and here are contained a series of recommended actions which will allow that journey to be made. As has already been stated, the Buddha was more interested in practice than metaphysical speculation, and what is listed here are practical measures which if employed have an utterly transformative effect. They are measures that should be adopted by those who wish to free themselves from the cycle of samsara, the cycle of life and death.

Although the Buddha taught that there is, in the final analysis, no individual identity as such, those things to which we devote ourselves have a karmic effect on future lives which arise 'like one fire lit from another'.

When looking at the Eightfold Path it becomes evident that the eight may be divided into three distinct areas of life, areas that were of particular concern to the Buddha. These are wisdom, morality and meditation.

Wisdom involves Right View or coming to a proper understanding of the truth of the Buddha's teaching. All of us have had an insight, a flash of understanding, when our view suddenly changes. With that flash arises the realization that life as we know it has its limitations. In moments of greater awareness the sense of separation normally experienced gives way to a deep appreciation of the underlying unity, a unity from which we are in no way separate. From this experience there may arise a resolution to come to a deeper and more lasting understanding of the true nature of things. This is Right Resolve, and as part of this resolution there may arise the steady determination to meet and counter those deep ingrained habits of heart and mind that force us into a state of separation and suffering. Involving both heart and mind, the decision to be made is both emotional and intellectual. This is the second aspect of wisdom.

Morality involves speech, action and the way we gain our livelihood. Right Speech concerns the truth, holding the words of truth in mind, and speaking from that truth in a way that is true. This doesn't mean that these words remain as a set of ideas but are the words of truth discovered in experience and spoken in a way that causes no harm.

Words are all important. Our experience of the world is forged out of the ideas that we carry with us. If we avoid not only lying to others but also lying to ourselves, everything will not only be freed from the distortions we have imposed but will become purified and therefore more translucent and luminous.

Right Action is a direct result of refined ideas. If our words are of the nature of greed, hatred and delusion then must our action be likewise. How different are actions that arise out of their opposites: generosity, compassion and understanding. These are skilful actions which are quite different from the clumsy results of egotistical prompting. Actions such as these, because of the limits placed upon them by the nature of their source, are bound to be mistimed and mis-measured, and rather than unify and resolve, will inevitably create division. Skilful actions, which draw together and break down division, come from an altogether different source and have an altogether different quality.

Right Livelihood encourages us to seek a way of sustaining ourselves which minimizes the impact we have on others and the world. In gaining our living we may feel that circumstances force us into ignoring such considerations, but Right Livelihood encourages us to think differently, to appreciate the interconnectedness of all things and to tread lightly with care.

The third main area dealt with in the Eightfold Path is meditation. This is not surprising given that Siddhartha became the Buddha through single pointed meditation. He resolved to attain Enlightenment. He sat upon the ground and swore that 'Flesh may wither, blood may dry up, but I shall not leave this seat until I gain Enlightenment!' Such resolution is therefore an essential part of the meditative process, to remain undeflected and undeterred regardless of the difficulties encountered. Inevitably there are mental traits, deep ingrained habits of heart and mind which need to be countered with steady determination.

Right Mindfulness is one of the great joys of the reflective life. When we adopt mindfulness we immediately allow for quiet observation; the possibility that, rather than being utterly identified with all the thoughts and feelings which rise in the heart and mind, we have the capacity to stand back and quietly observe the promptings of self-identification. What Mindfulness also does is draw us out of all the concerns for the past and future, all the confusion that arises out of a self-created imaginary world, and to bring us back to the immediate reality of the here and now. To be dominated by thoughts and feelings which are in a state of constant flux is not a way of bringing steadiness and consistency to our actions. The movements of the mind are many; the unidentified observer is unitary, therefore, calm and clear.

Calmness and clarity are much desired, but personal desire will never provide them. Desire has the opposite effect. It agitates rather than calms. It confuses rather than clarifies. But as has already been stated, quiet determination is another thing. It involves laying aside all wishes for oneself, giving up this little self and recognising it for what it is, a matrix of elements. It is not therefore some kind of personal attainment that is being sought in meditation, but rather a dissolution of all that holds us confined. Remember the Buddha's own experience watching his father ploughing whilst he sat in the shade of a rose-apple tree, of how he quite naturally slipped below the surface of life and discovered 'Enlightenment'. It is about dissolving and merging, the key ingredients of the reflective life. And it is reflection that is being offered by this book, words to be carried into daily life, to be held in mind as an oasis of peace and bliss.

Although the daily reflections which follow are drawn primarily from the Pali Texts which formed the original corpus of Buddhist thinking, even those that are not are much respected and therefore in accord with the Buddha's original teaching. The very fact that the texts have been chosen for reflection is very much in keeping with the Buddha's avowed purpose, not speculation but transformation. As has already been stressed, Buddhism is a practical philosophy. These texts are for a practical purpose.

To reflect upon the words of the Buddha, to allow them to suffuse the heart and mind is a time-honoured way of coming to a true understanding of what is meant. This is not theoretical understanding – yet more ideas to add to the general stock of information we already possess. Reflecting upon these texts will allow there to arise a deeper understanding of how to live in harmony and not discord, in unity and not division, in Truth and not delusion.

Carry the book with you or write one of the thoughts for continual reference. Many of these texts were learnt by heart and passed on from generation to generation. Why not follow suit and learn some of them by heart, especially those that have a particular resonance? Rather than making up your mind as to their meaning, hold them in mind and allow their significance to have its effect on the way you experience life.

Standing or walking,
sitting or lying down,
during all these waking hours,
let him establish mindfulness of good
will, which men call the highest state!

'When you spoke of
wholesome dharmas which
ones did you mean?'
'I meant morality,
faith, vigour, mindfulness
and concentration.'

Watchful amongst the unwatchful,
awake amongst those that sleep,
the wise man like a swift horse
runs his race, outrunning
those who are slow.

What we are today comes
from our thoughts of yesterday,
and present thoughts build
our life of tomorrow:
our life is the creation of our mind.

He who for the sake of
happiness hurts others who
also want happiness, shall not
hereafter find happiness.

When faith arises it arrests
the Five Hindrances and the heart becomes free
from them, clear, serene and undisturbed.

Never speak harsh words,
for once spoken they may return to you.
Angry words are painful and there
may be blows for blows.

To neglect the highest
dharma, and instead to
think demeritorious thoughts,
is like neglecting the jewels on
the jewel-island and collecting
lumps of earth instead.

The wise do not take delight in
the senses and their objects,
are not impressed by them,
are not attached to them and
in consequence their craving ceases.

If a man speaks or
acts with a pure mind,
joy follows him
as his own shadow.

Hate is not
conquered by hate:
hate is conquered by love.
This is a law eternal.

This contemplation is one which I, mindful, enter upon and mindful emerge from.

Who passion and hate and ignorance
have left, him they call one who
has made the self become,
who is Brahma-become,
truth finder, an awakened one,
who's passed by fear and dread,
one who has abandoned
everything.

For whatever a man
thinks about continually,
to that his mind
becomes inclined by
force of habit.

Men who are foolish and ignorant are
careless and never watchful;
but the man who lives in watchfulness
considers it his greatest treasure.

This dharma I teach is deep,
difficult to see, difficult to understand,
peaceful, excellent, beyond dialectic,
subtle, intelligible to the wise.

Never surrender to carelessness;
never sink into weak pleasures
and lust. Those who are watchful,
in deep contemplation, reach
the end, the joy supreme.

A brightly shining fire, when not stirred by the wind, is soon appeased; so the unstimulated heart of those who live in seclusion wins peace without much effort.

Hidden in the mystery
of consciousness, the mind,
incorporeal, flies alone
far away. Those who set
their mind on harmony
become free from the
bonds of death.

A person who is neither tempter of self nor a
tormentor of others is, in this very life,
stilled, attained to nirvana, become cool;
he is one who experiences bliss; he lives with
a self that has become Brahma.

As a mountain peak is inaccessible, so is nirvana inaccessible to all passions. As no seed can grow on a mountain peak, so the seeds of all the passions cannot grow in nirvana.

The mind is wavering and restless,
difficult to guard and restrain.
Let the wise man straighten his mind
as a maker of arrows makes
his arrow straight.

A mind which is not
protected by mindfulness
is as helpless as a
blind man walking over
uneven ground without
a guide.

As the bee takes the essence of
a flower and flies away without
destroying its beauty and perfume,
so let the sage wander in this life.

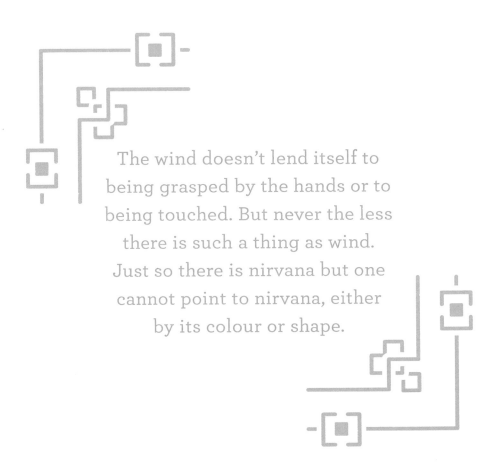

The wind doesn't lend itself to being grasped by the hands or to being touched. But never the less there is such a thing as wind. Just so there is nirvana but one cannot point to nirvana, either by its colour or shape.

For those following
the stream of becoming,
who are overcome by touches?
Proceeding by the false way,
distant is the destruction
of the fetters.

The wrong action seems sweet
to the fool until the reaction comes and brings
pain, and the bitter fruits of wrong deeds have then
to be eaten by the fool.

Arise (from sloth), sir (meditating);
train swiftly for tranquility.
Let not death's king find you proud,
nor dupe you to subjection.

Slothfulness is dust...
Being prone to it is dust:
by diligence, by knowledge,
draw out the barb of self.

And if to his own harm the fool increases in cleverness, this only destroys his own mind, and his fate is worse than before.

Look upon the man who tells thee thy faults as if he told thee of hidden treasure, the wise man who shows thee the dangers of life. Follow that man: he who follows him will see good and not evil.

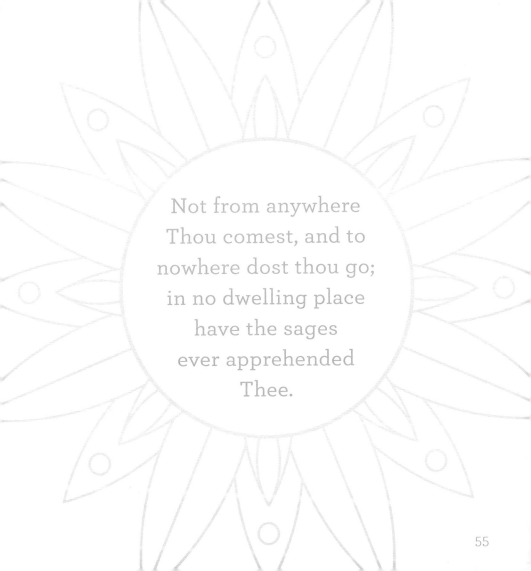

Not from anywhere
Thou comest, and to
nowhere dost thou go;
in no dwelling place
have the sages
ever apprehended
Thee.

Have not for friends those
whose soul is ugly; go not
with men who have an evil soul.
Have for friends those whose
soul is beautiful; go with
men whose soul is good.

If your sense-organs are calm,
so will the acts of the body become calm,
calm the acts of speech,
calm the acts of mind; and one
may think: 'We will offer an
offering – calm itself – to our
fellow Brahma-farers.'

Learn this from the river's flow
in mountain cleft and chasm:
loud gush the rivulets,
the great stream silent moves.
Loud booms the empty thing.
The full is ever calm;
like pot half-full the fool,
like full pot the sage.

Who knows and
curbed-of-self, tho' knowing,
speaks not much:
the sage and wisdom
worths, that sage still
wisdom wins.

Just as a flower which seems beautiful
and has colour but has no perfume,
so are the fruitless words
of the man who speaks them
but does them not.

As all plants and animals which increase
and grow and prosper, do so with the earth
as their support, with the earth as their basis,
just so the Yogin, with morality as his support,
with morality as his basis, develops the
five cardinal virtues:
faith, vigour, mindfulness,
concentration and wisdom.

From the utter fading away
and stopping of ignorance the constructions
stop, and so stops each of the rest. Such is
the stopping of this entire mass of ill.

Joy is born in one who has delight,
the body of one who has joy is calmed,
one whose body is calmed feels ease,
and the mind of one who is at ease
is contemplative.

Overcome anger by peacefulness: overcome evil by good. Overcome the mean by generosity; and the man who lies by truth.

The Brahma-faring is lived for the advantage of the training, for the further wisdom, for the essence of freedom, for mastery in mindfulness.

Those who are forever watchful,
who study themselves day and night,
and who wholly strive for nirvana,
all their passions pass away.

The Great Way is calm
and large hearted,
for it nothing is easy,
nothing hard.

The man who controls his senses as a good driver controls his horses, and who is free from lower passions and pride, is admired even by the gods.

He is calm like the earth that endures;
he is steady like a column that is firm;
he is pure like a lake that is clear;
he is free from samsara,
the ever-returning life-in-death.

Better than a thousand useless words is one word that gives peace.

Obey the nature of things,
and you are in concord with
The Way, calm and easy and
free from annoyance.

If a man should conquer in battle
a thousand and thousand more,
and another should conquer himself,
his would be the greater victory,
because the greatest of victories is
the victory over oneself.

Stopping of
becoming
is nirvana.

'He insulted me, he hurt me,
he defeated me, he robbed me.'
Those who think such things
will not be free from hate.

Pursue not the outer entanglements,
dwell not on the Inner Void;
be serene in the oneness of things,
and dualism vanishes by itself.

Through perseverance,
vigilance and self-restraint,
a wise person creates a safe harbour
for herself that no storm
can overwhelm.

As from a large heap of flowers many
garlands and wreaths are made, so
by a mortal in this
life there is much good
work to be done.

The wise one does not judge others, not their words or deeds or what they have or have not done. The wise one only contemplates her own words and deeds.

How long is the night to the watchman; how long is the road to the weary; how long is the wandering of lives ending in death for the fool who cannot find the path!

Deeds done in harmony
with one's path of life are
those which bring
clarity and peace and
harmony to the doer.

Those who make channels for water control the water; makers of arrows make the arrows straight; carpenters control their timber; and the wise control their own minds.

Whosoever honours in reverence those
who are old in virtue and holiness,
he indeed conquers four treasures:
long life and health, and power and joy.

There is an unborn,
un-become, unmade, incomposite,
and were there not, there would
be no escape from the born,
the become, the made and
the composite world.

Better than a hundred years
lived in ignorance, without contemplation,
is one single day of life lived in wisdom
and deep contemplation.

Better than a hundred years lived
in idleness and in weakness is a single
day of life lived with courage and
powerful striving.

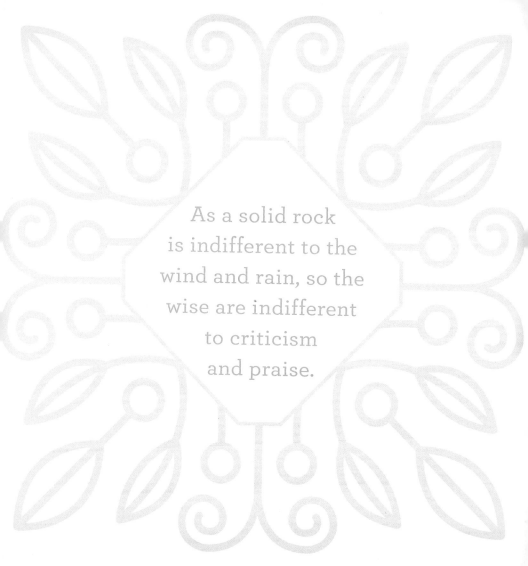

As a solid rock
is indifferent to the
wind and rain, so the
wise are indifferent
to criticism
and praise.

A man may find pleasure in evil as long as his evil has not given fruit; but when the fruit of evil comes then that man finds evil indeed.

Abandon the ways of confusion and darkness and live in the light of peace and harmony.

Have fire like a noble horse
touched by the whip.
By faith, by virtue,
by wisdom and by right
action, you shall overcome
the sorrows of life.

The moment we
are enlightened within,
we go beyond the
voidness of a world
confronting us.

Hold not a sin of little worth,
thinking 'this is little to me'.
The falling of drops of water
will in time fill a water-jar.
Even so the foolish man
becomes full of evil although
he gather it little by little.

O let us live in joy,
in peace amongst those
who struggle!
Among men who struggle,
let us live in peace.

If you can be in silent quietness like a broken gong that is silent, you have reached the peace of nirvana and your anger is peace.

He who for himself or others
craves not for sons or power or
wealth, who puts not his own success
before the success of righteousness,
he is virtuous, and righteous
and wise.

If a man does something wrong,
let him not do it again and again.
Let him find no pleasure in his sin.
Painful is the accumulation
of wrongdoings.

One who values happiness
for himself but creates anxiety
for others is confused.

The man
who has no evil
cannot be hurt
by evil.

Let him be strenuous, upright and truly straight,
without conceit of self, easily contented and joyous,
free of cares; let him not be submerged by things
of this world; let him not take upon the burden of
worldly goods; let his senses be controlled; let him
be wise, not puffed up and let him not desire great
possessions even for his family. Let him do nothing
that is mean or that the wise would reprove.

Self-applause, belittling others,
or encouragement to sin,
some such evil's sure to happen where
one fool meets another.

Consciousness
is unending.

Think not of the faults of others,
of what they have done or not done.
Think rather of your own sins,
of the things you have done
or not done.

Even as on a heap of rubbish thrown away by the side of the road, a lotus flower may grow and blossom with its pure perfume giving joy to the soul, in the same way among the blind multitudes shines pure the light of wisdom of the student who follows the Buddha, the One who is truly awake.

What is clinging? There are four kinds of clinging: Clinging to pleasure. Clinging to views. Clinging to rules, techniques and vows. Clinging to self.

He who in early days was unwise but later found wisdom, he sheds light over the world like that of the moon when free from clouds.

I am the result of my own deeds, heir to deeds.
Whatever deed I do, whether good or evil, I shall
become its heir. This should be
contemplated often.

Abandoning what is unwholesome, you ought to ponder what is wholesome, for that will bring you advantages in this world and help you to win the heighest goal.

Better than power over all the
earth, better than going to
heaven and better than dominion
over the worlds is the joy of the
man who enters the river of life
that leads to nirvana.

When desires
go, joy comes.
The follower of
Buddha finds
this truth.

Drench, pervade, fill and pervade this body itself with zest and ease that are born of contemplation.

Not to hurt by deeds of words,
self-control as taught in the Rules, moderation in
food, the solitude of one's room and one's bed, and
the practice of the highest consciousness: this is
the teachings of the Buddhas who are awake.

If ill-will or the desire
to hurt others should stir
your mind, purify it with the
opposite. Friendliness and
compassion are their antidotes;
for they are as ever as
opposed to hatred as light
to darkness.

He who does what should
not be done, who forgets the
true aim of life and sinks
into transient pleasures –
he will one day envy the
man who lives in
high contemplation.

'This is myself and this is another.'
Be free of this bond which encompasses
you about, and your own self is
thereby released.

To strive for purity of vision, and yet be
blinded by faulty judgement – that prolongs
the bondage.

When a man knows the solitude of silence, and feels the joy of quietness, he is then free from fear and he feels the joy of the dharma.

There are four bases
of sympathy: charity,
kind speech, doing a
good turn and treating
all alike.

Consumed by wisdom, faults cease to thrive and grow, like a tree which flares up after it has been struck by a thunderbolt.

He whose vision is deep, who is wise,
who knows the path and
what is outside the path, who has
attained the highest end –
him I call a Brahmin.

The conqueror gets
one who conquers him;
Th' abuser wins abuse,
thus by evolution of the deed
a man that spoils is
spoiled in his turn.

All material shapes, feelings, perceptions,
constructions, and all consciousness,
whether past, future or present, subjective or
objective, gross or subtle, mean or excellent,
near or far, must all be seen as:
this is not mine, I am not this, this is not myself.

He who in his vision is
free from doubts and,
having all, longs for
nothing, for he has
reached immortal freedom –
him call I a Brahmin.

If acts of thought are done through love
towards his fellows in the Brahma-faring,
both openly and in private – this is a matter
which conduces to unity.

Let him first find
what is right and then
he can teach it to
others, thus avoiding
useless pain.

Do not trivialize small acts of peace and harmony, thinking, 'I will never reap what I have sown'. A pitcher is filled one drop of water at a time and a person centred in oneness who proceeds in peace and harmony will soon manifest the peace and harmony in his life.

If one abandons onslaught on creatures, abstains from it, lays aside stick, lays aside knife, he lives modest, merciful, compassionate towards all living creatures. He is not crooked in body, speech, thought.

The self is
not in Self.

The end remains untold.

Each of the Sayings was derived from the following Buddhist texts:

Anguttara-Nikaya
Bodhicaryavatara
Buddhacarita
Bya chos
Digha-Nikaya
Diamond Sutra
Digh-Nakaya
Dhammapada
Dohakosha
Doctrinal texts collected by C. Humphries
Itivuttka
Jatakamala
Majahima-Nikaya
Milindapanha
On Hakuin's Zazen Wasan
Papancasudani
Prajnaparamitastotrha
Samyuyutta-Nikaya
Sessan Amakuki
Sin sin ming
Sutanipata
Udana
Vinaya-Pitaka
Visuddhimagga

Arcturus Publishing Limited have made every reasonable effort to ensure that all permissions information has been sought and achieved as required. However there may be inadvertent and occasional errors in seeking permission to reproduce individual Sayings for which Arcturus Publishing Limited apologizes. If you are the Copyright owner of any such entry please contact Arcturus directly so we may add the necessary reference and acknowledgement.